GLASS

Hazel Songhurst

Consultants: Pilkington Glass Consultants

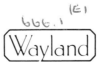

Titles in this series

Bricks
Glass
Paper

Plastics
Water
Wood

Cover: (Main picture) Molten glass slides down these tubes into moulds at the bottom where air is blown in to make them into bottles. (Top right) Drinking glasses.

Editor: Sarah Doughty

First published in 1991 by
Wayland (Publishers) Ltd
61 Western Road, Hove
East Sussex, BN3 1JD, England

British Library Cataloguing in Publication Data
Songhurst, Hazel
   Glass.
   1. Glass
   I. Title   II. Series
   666.1

ISBN 0 7502 0154 1

Typeset by Dorchester Typesetting Group Ltd
Printed in Italy by G. Canale & C.S.p.A.
Bound in Belgium by Casterman S.A.

Contents

All the words that appear in
bold are explained in
the glossary on page 30.

What is glass?

Glass is one of the most important **materials** we have. Glass was discovered a very long time ago, and has been used for centuries to make useful objects. Look around you and see how many things are made of glass. Windows, mirrors, bottles, jars, lenses and television screens are all made of glass.

Glass is usually a hard, **brittle** material. But when glass is heated it changes. The glass melts, and runs and flows like a sticky liquid.

A long ribbon of hot, liquid glass flows on to a conveyor belt in the glass factory.

4

Molten glass can be pulled, stretched and pressed in any direction and made into different shapes.

Glass is a strong, hard material that is made into objects of all shapes and sizes.

When glass is cool, it becomes strong and hard. The glass may feel solid, but it is still really a liquid. Scientists call glass a 'supercooled liquid'. Like a clear liquid, glass is **transparent** and light passes through it. The unusual properties of glass make it a very useful material.

How glass is made

Clear glass is made mostly from **silica sand.** This is a very pure, clean type of sand. The other ingredients are **soda ash** and **limestone**. To make glass, they are all mixed together and melted in a **furnace** at a temperature of 1,500 °C.

Glass can be made by just using silica sand, but it needs a much higher heat to melt it.

To make glass, silica sand, soda ash and limestone are melted together in a furnace.

Left Silica sand piled up outside the glass factory. This is the main ingredient for glass.

Below Heavy lead-crystal glass is made by adding the metal lead to the glass mixture.

So soda ash is used to make the mixture melt at a lower temperature. Adding limestone stops the finished glass from breaking up in water. Suitable waste glass is also added to the ingredients. This makes the glass mixture melt more quickly.

Different types of glass can be made by adding to the glass mixture. Adding **lead** makes a heavy lead-crystal glass that is used to make wine glasses. Adding **borax** makes a glass that can be heated safely, and is used for making test-tubes or pots and pans for cooking.

7

Blowing glass

The glass-maker heats the glass in a small furnace to stop it hardening while being shaped.

In the past, all glass was blown and shaped by hand. It is a skill that is still used today, and glass-makers blow glass to make beautiful and unusual objects.

To blow glass, the glass-maker blows down a long, hollow metal rod which has a lump of molten glass on the end. The molten glass forms a bubble and is shaped against a stone slab.

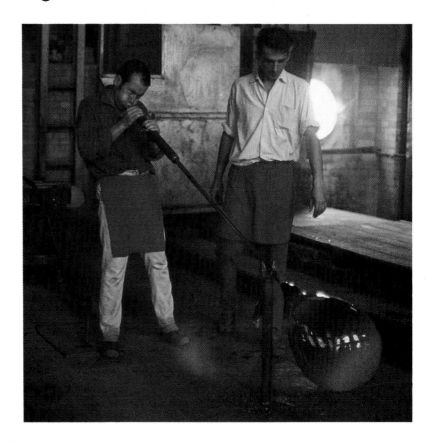

The glass-maker blows down the hollow rod to make the lump of glass on the end into a bubble.

The glass-maker uses tools to cut and shape the handle of this glass vase.

The glass-maker cuts off the top of the bubble with shears, and finishes shaping the work with tools. He or she works quickly to shape the glass while it is still hot. Finally the glass-maker breaks off the metal rod and leaves the glass to cool and harden.

Today, ordinary glass jars and bottles are still made by blowing glass, but it is usually done in a factory by machines that use **compressed air**.

Glass for bottles

Glass is used to package all kinds of food and drink. This is because it is strong, easy to clean and does not leak. Computers work out the best shape for a bottle or jar and how much glass to use.

Bottles and jars are made by blowing glass. The glass is blown **automatically**. To make a bottle, a lump of molten glass called a **gob** is dropped into a mould.

This diagram shows how molten glass is put into moulds and blown to make a bottle.

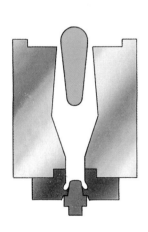

Molten glass drops into mould

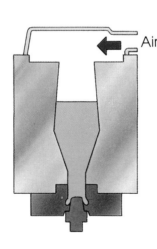

Air

Air is blown in from the top to make the neck

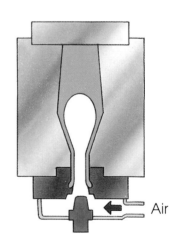

Air

Air is blown in at the bottom to make the rough shape

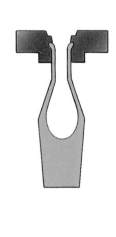

Bottle shape is formed

Air is then blown in, forcing it into a rough shape called a **parison**.

The parison is then put into a second mould and more air is blown in to make the final shape. The glass bottle is then reheated and cooled very slowly inside a long tunnel called a **lehr**. This is called **annealing**.

The new bottles are carefully checked before being sent to a bottling **plant**. Here they are filled and sealed and given a label.

Above *Finished bottles are carefully checked for any faults.*

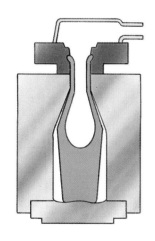

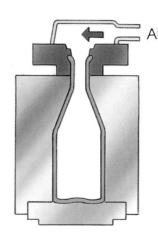

Air

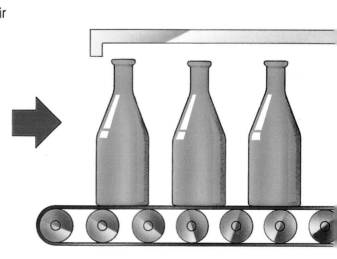

Bottle shape is placed in the second mould

Air is blown in the top to make the finished shape

Annealing lehr for heating and cooling bottles

Making flat glass

The most common use for glass is for windows. This is because it is strong, clear and weatherproof. But for hundreds of years, making big pieces of flat glass was difficult and costly.

Today flat glass is cheap and easy to make using the **float glass** method. This was discovered by the British company Pilkington in 1959. Hot molten glass is floated on the top of molten tin in a large tank. The smooth surface of the tin makes the molten glass layer flat. The glass is made thicker or thinner by changing the speed the glass flows through the tank.

This diagram shows the different stages for making flat glass.

Glass ingredients

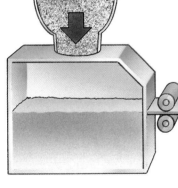

Melting furnace

Glass floating on molten tin

Annealing lehr (heating and cooling in oven)

The flat glass is then heated and cooled very slowly. This is the annealing process and takes place in the long tunnel called the lehr. The flat glass is moved along rollers to where it is automatically washed, cut into big sheets and stacked.

Left A long ribbon of cooled flat glass comes out of the lehr to be washed and cut.

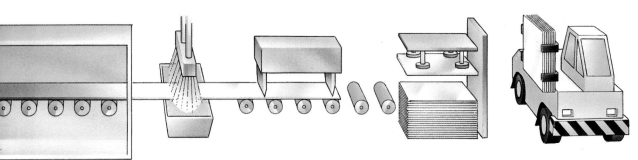

Washing   Cutting   Stacking   Transporting to warehouse

Glass in buildings

In the past, most buildings had windows with small panes of thick, bumpy glass that did not let in much light. Today new buildings are built with big windows to let in plenty of light. This makes rooms look cheerful and spacious.

Many windows in buildings today are **double-glazed**. This gives good protection against the weather. The walls of some high-rise blocks are made of solar-control glass panels. They are made by altering the ingredients of ordinary glass or covering glass panels with a layer of metal or colour coating. This lets the light in, but absorbs or reflects the heat. This keeps the rooms inside cool on the hottest day.

Shop display windows are made from big sheets of glass. It is best to use special safety glass in places where there are lots of people because ordinary glass breaks so easily.

It is best to use strengthened glass for shop windows in busy streets.

This skyscraper in Canada has solar-control glass panel walls.

Decorative glass

Squeezing glass between rollers. The top roller has a pattern cut into it.

Glass is made with different patterns and colours. See how many different kinds of decorative glass you can find at home on doors, windows, bowls and vases.

A decoration for fine glass can be made by cutting it on the edge of a fast-moving copper wheel. A sharp point can also be used to scratch the glass surface to make a pattern. Lead glass is often used because it is soft to cut and sparkles in the light.

This craftsman is cutting a pattern on a glass bowl using a sharp copper wheel.

16

A pattern can be made on hot glass by pressing it between metal rollers. This makes the glass into a flat sheet. The top roller has a pattern cut into it, which is rolled on to the glass.

Coloured glass has been used for centuries to make beautiful decorations. The glass is coloured by adding metals like copper or iron to the glass mixture before it is heated. Stained glass windows are made up of small panes of coloured glass. These are **soldered** into lead frames to make very beautiful pictures.

Stained glass windows are made of shapes of coloured glass that are fixed together with lead strips

Making glass stronger

When ordinary glass breaks it smashes into dangerous, jagged pieces. This can be dangerous so special types of safety glass are made.

The first safety glass to be made was wired glass. This glass has a wire **mesh** which is laid between the two sheets of glass. If a building with wired glass in the windows catches fire, the melted glass does not fall, but stays stuck to the wire mesh.

Above Wired safety glass.

A smashed windscreen that does not fall into sharp pieces.

To make laminated glass, a clear plastic sheet is sandwiched between two layers of flat glass.

Toughened glass is made using a very high heat so that it is stronger than ordinary glass. Car windscreens are often made from toughened glass. If the windscreen breaks, it falls apart in small lumps with no sharp edges.

The strongest glass is called laminated glass. A clear plastic layer, or laminate is laid between two layers of glass. If the glass breaks the pieces of glass stay fixed to the plastic. Aircraft windscreens which need to be very strong are often made of laminated glass.

Looking at lenses

Lenses are pieces of curved glass. When you look through a lens, the curved shape of the glass changes the way you see things. This is very useful as it can make things look bigger or smaller.

Some lenses have thick glass in the middle. This makes an object look bigger than it actually is. These are called convex lenses. Other lenses are thin in the middle and make things look smaller. These are concave lenses.

If you look at an object through a convex lens it makes what you see appear bigger. This is its virtual image.

If you look at an object through a concave lens it makes what you see appear smaller. This is its virtual image.

20

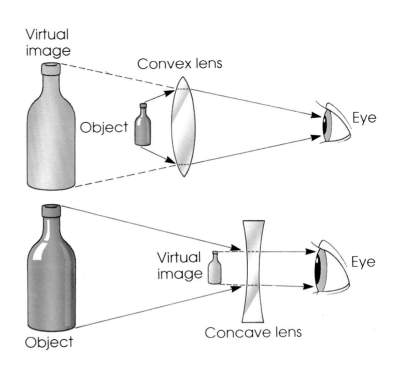

Virtual image

Convex lens

Object

Eye

Virtual image

Object

Concave lens

Eye

The magnifying glass makes the plant look bigger so it can be seen more clearly.

Lenses are made from **optical glass**. Hot molten glass is pressed into shapes called **blanks**. These are carefully ground and polished to the exact size and thickness that is needed.

Lenses are used in cameras, binoculars, telescopes and microscopes. People with bad eyesight wear glasses. The lens is made to the right shape and thickness to help them to see better.

Mirrors

A mirror gives us a **reflection** of what it 'sees'. Glass is used for making mirrors. This glass has a thin layer of silver on one side. This shiny metal reflects light.

The glass that is used to make a mirror needs to be very flat. This is because small curves in the glass alter the reflection you see. Perhaps you have looked in mirrors at fairgrounds where wavy glass is used to make crazy reflections.

Wavy glass mirrors at a fairground pull and stretch this girl's reflection out of shape.

To make a mirror, first the sheet of glass is carefully washed. It is then covered with layers of tin and silver and a copper coating to protect it. When they have dried, the coated side of the glass is covered with two layers of special paint for protection.

Mirrors have lots of uses. They are often used in buildings to make rooms look bigger, or are tinted and used on the outside as solar-control glass. Some telescopes use big mirrors to reflect light from the stars. A **solar furnace** uses mirrors to trap and reflect the sun's heat.

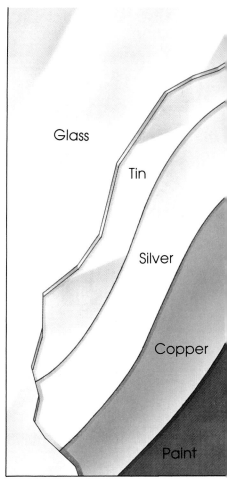

Above This diagram shows the layers that cover a glass sheet to make a mirror.

Left The huge mirror traps the sun's rays to make energy to work a furnace.

23

Glass that bends

Glass is a hard, rigid material that breaks easily. But if molten glass is forced through tiny holes it can be pulled into fine, soft threads of glass that bend easily.

These threads of glass are called glass fibre. They can be made into thick matting and used for **insulation**. You may have glass fibre in the walls and roof of your home. Glass fibre is useful because it keeps buildings warm in winter and cool in summer.

These men have put glass fibre into the walls of a new house to insulate it.

Glass fibre can be mixed with other materials to make the material stronger. If glass fibre is mixed with plastic it makes 'glass reinforced plastic' often called GRP. This is used to make car bodies and boat hulls because it is strong and waterproof. If glass fibre is mixed with cement it makes 'glass reinforced concrete' or GRC. This is a strong material that is often used for building.

Glass reinforced plastic is light and strong. The bodies of Lotus cars are made of this material.

Recycling glass

Glass lasts a long time. Glass bottles can be used again and again. But very often glass is used only once and thrown away. This is a waste of a useful material. It also harms the environment because glass does not break down but remains in the earth forever.

Many people are very concerned about this. In some countries nearly half of the bottles that are used are **recycled**. They are taken to special places called

This diagram shows what happens to glass at a recycling centre.

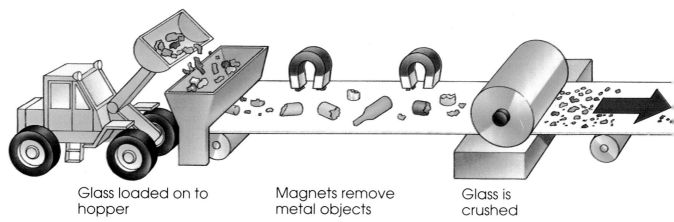

Glass loaded on to hopper

Magnets remove metal objects

Glass is crushed

bottle banks. At a bottle bank, containers are used to collect brown, clear and green glass. A lorry picks up the glass and takes it to a recycling centre. Here the glass is washed and crushed up into pieces.

At the glass factory the crushed glass is added to the glass mixture in the furnace. The glass is melted. Remelting glass uses up much less energy than melting new materials. At the same time, smaller amounts of new materials are needed to make glass. In this way the world's resources are being saved by recycling glass.

Above Bottle banks help people to recycle glass.

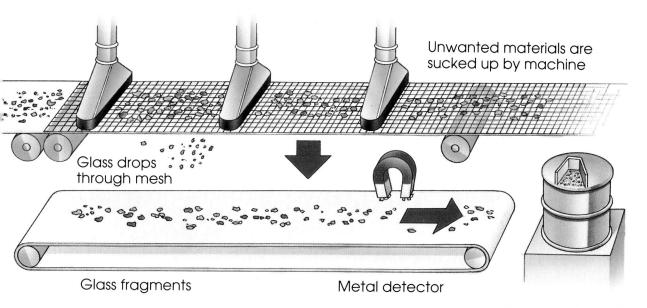

Unwanted materials are sucked up by machine

Glass drops through mesh

Glass fragments

Metal detector

Glass stored ready to go to glass factory

Projects with glass

Musical glass

You will need:

Empty glass bottles of different shapes
Water

A spoon
Drinking glasses

1. Fill some empty bottles with water. Lightly tap the bottles with a spoon to make notes. Vary the amounts of water to make low and high notes.

2. Collect different shaped bottles – some with short thick necks, others with long necks. Try blowing across the tops of them to make sounds. Which shape bottles work best?

3. Wet your finger and rub it round the rim of different sized drinking glasses. Can you produce a note? Which is the most musical glass – is it thick or thin glass?

Make a 'stained glass window'

You will need:

Coloured acetate
Black sticky tape
Pencil, paper and scissors

1. Draw a picture or pattern on paper. Keep this design very simple. It is best to draw big, angular shapes. Cut out your paper design and keep all the pieces in position.

2. Use these paper shapes as a pattern to cut out acetate shapes in different colours.

3. Arrange the cut-out shapes on to a flat surface in position. Make sure they fit well together. Join the pieces with black sticky tape.

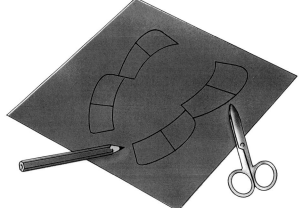

4. Position your 'stained glass' on a sunny window and stick down with tape.

If you hold up a sheet of white paper in front of your 'stained glass' you will see coloured spots of light reflected on to the paper. On a dull day, shine a torch through to show this effect.

Glossary

Annealing   The slow re-heating and cooling of glass.

Automatic   When something can work by itself, such as a machine.

Blank   A partially-shaped piece of glass made by pressing or blowing.

Borax   A mineral that is added to make a very tough glass.

Brittle   Breaks easily.

Compressed air   Air that is squeezed so that it is at a very high pressure.

Double-glazed   Two layers of glass fitted in a window.

Float glass   Flat clear glass made by allowing molten glass to float on tin.

Furnace   An enclosed place that produces a very high heat.

Gob   A lump of a soft substance such as melted glass.

Insulation   A material that stops the movement of cold or warm air through the walls or roof of a building.

Lead   A heavy metal.

Lehr   An oven where newly-made glass is slowly heated and cooled.

Limestone   A chalky rock which is used in glass-making.

Material   A substance that is used to make something else.

Mesh   A network of wire.

Molten glass   Hot, melted liquid glass.

Optical glass   A pure, very high-quality clear glass used to make lenses.

Parison   The name given to the first shape of a bottle or jar.

Plant   A factory or works where industry takes place.

Recycled   When materials that have been used are treated so that they can be used again.

Reflection   When light is thrown back from a surface so that you can see an image.

Silica sand   The main ingredient of glass. It is found naturally in sand as a material called quartz.

Soda ash   A material used in glass-making that is made in a chemical factory.

Solar furnace   A furnace that uses mirrors to trap the sun's rays as a source of heat.

Soldered Joined together by heat or pressure.

Transparent   A material that allows light to pass through so you can see through it.

Books to read

Cackett, S. **Glass** (Franklin Watts, 1988)
Chandler, J. **Glass** (A & C Black, 1988)
Paterson, A.J. **Glass** (Faber & Faber, 1985)
Rickard, G. **Focus on Glass** (Wayland, 1988)

Useful addresses

Australia
ACI Fibreglass
Frankston Road
Dandenong. VIC.3175

Federated Glass Merchants
  Association of Australia
100 Drummond Street
Carlton. VIC.3122

Canada
Consumer's Glass
777 Kipling Avenue
Toronto, Ontario
M8Z 524

Glass Trades Association of
  Northern Alberta
121 Cedar Street
Sherwood, Alberta
T8A 2E7

UK
British Glass
Northumberland Road
Sheffield S10 2UA

Pilkington Glass Museum
Prescot Road
St Helen's, Liverpool
Merseyside WA10 3TT

USA

National China and Glass
  Giftware Association
1115 Clifton Avenue
Clifton, New Jersey

National Glass Association
8200 Greensboro Drive
302 McClean
Virginia 22102

Index

Picture acknowledgements

The publishers would like to thank the following for allowing their photographs to be reproduced in this book: British Glass 7 (bottom), 16 (bottom); Bruce Coleman Ltd (Fco Márquez) 8 (top), (Jen and Des Bartlett) 18; Greg Evans Photo Library 15, 23; Eye Ubiquitous (John Hulme) 22; Chris Fairclough Colour Library *title page*, 21, 24; Pilkington plc 6, 13, 16 (top), 19; Schott Glass Ltd 4, 7 (top), 8 (bottom), 9, 11, 17; Topham Picture Library *cover* (top), 5; Stephen White-Thomson 27; Zefa *cover* (bottom), 14, 25. All artwork by Peter Bull Art except for page 18 by the Hayward Art Group and pages 28-9 by Janos Marffi.